Sesi

A S African Woman of God

GoGo Mona Lea

WestBow Press books may be ordered through booksellers or by contacting:

WestBow Press
A Division of Thomas Nelson & Zondervan
1663 Liberty Drive
Bloomington, IN 47403
www.westbowpress.com
1 (866) 928-1240

ISBN: 978-1-9736-9451-9 (sc)
ISBN: 978-1-9736-9450-2 (e)

Library of Congress Control Number: 2020911815

Print information available on the last page.

WestBow Press rev. date: 7/2/2020

WESTBOW
PRESS®
A DIVISION OF THOMAS NELSON
& ZONDERVAN

Acknowledgements

I want to thank Kim, Elijah, Uncle Sikanda and the rest of their talented staff and teachers for welcoming me with open arms. Their love for Christ and following the school's mantra was evident.

I was not able to get all the teachers and helpers' pictures. Uncle Emmanuel, Sarah, Mama Kedi (Beauty's mother), Tuflos (chauffer and 'all around' helper), Claudia, Gao (Magdalene), Nora, and Mosky, who tried to teach me Africanos language – I failed.

My sincere apologies to all. These are all people of equal importance to Dayspring and friends of Sesi's – and now mine. I also now have 92 'adopted' children.

I also wish to thank my typist, computer whiz, encourager and friend – Pat Murphy.

Thanks also to the capable staff at Westbow Press who patiently walked me through all the steps to get the actual story to book form.

I am sitting here wondering how can I write a story about how a South African woman lives and gives God the glory each day?

Clearly, I can't, so, I'm going to just talk with Sesi and let her tell her own story. Sound fair?

I was born June 15, 1973. Papa named me, but Mama said "no". In school she'll be Esther! It was a cold day when I was born, Mama said.

My father was a farm worker on a farm nearby. My parents were overprotective of their one "little chick". They wanted the best for me.

When Daddy walked me to school "I shined". When he heard I'd gotten good grades he'd kill a chicken for me for supper and we'd celebrate.

I attended two schools in first to twelve grades. Seaport first, then Brits.

I always loved to sing. Started to sing in primary school.

I didn't have playmates. Never knew my aunts or uncles. We were a small nucleus. Like Papa, Mama and I was protected too.

I was always a leader in each class.

I had a dream at eight or nine. "I asked God for wisdom, like Solomon and more about you, God." You will be a teacher. (I didn't know Christian schools existed!)

My pastor said you can be a Sunday School teacher! And I was. I had many children to teach in Sunday School. 15 – 16 of them.

But I still felt that there was more, I met Mama Kedi at the same church. 1997. She was teaching at a Christian school.

At Cyara, about that time, Auntie Wendy and Charles Paine were praying for some place to teach all these "little souls". They decided that school would be called H.I.S. (the Lord's). Soon a telegram came saying, "hurry to nearby place to get money sent by an anonymous donor to purchase land nearby. It had recently come up for sale. The money was exact amount needed to buy land! That's how Dayspring came into being essentially.

Uncle Charles really did not, at first, have a vision for school. It was Auntie Wendy who started H.I.S. church.

Barb and her husband were missionaries and they had a vision for the school, so they came and spoke with Charles and Auntie Wendy and convinced them to start a school. Charles had always just loved to preach. I phoned and Wendy was principal. July 19, 1997. Monday. I packed a small bag. No blanket, no nothing and told my Mama "I was going to teach." I took a bus to Heckport.

Charles was at one of two garages on road and would collect children in his car to take to school. So that day I met Charles and Auntie Kim at Dayspring.

I took one look at all of it and I just knew that was where God wanted me to be.

Charles set me down then and interviewed me – He said I couldn't just come and expect to teach! I said, "God wants me teach here!" Then he called my Pastor who said "Oh, she's already there?"

Then Charles asked me who I wanted to teach, and I said "Oh, the little ones!" (and I still do.)

I was fresh out of high school, but that's who I knew I should teach!

Wendy gave me the ACE training. That's how I started. The manuals were so excellent in teaching me how to get better and better at teaching.

Charles and Wendy's son and Barb's sons were children in school also.

About this time Charles named it H.I.S. – Harvest International School. The government wanted to shut it down saying, "we don't need another school!!" But, Charles said, "no, no, it's a church".

Then the whole thing burned down. Nine children were in school. Cyara was no more. It was about five miles from where Dayspring is now. So, after the school burned at Cyara and new land was purchased and in July 1997 I came, and Auntie Kim had come six months earlier in December of 1996.

God's plan – 26 acres – three hut houses, main house, boys' and girls' toilets, learning center, Auntie Kim's original house, Lapa (thatched roof, no sides), cottage house, long building (divided into classrooms) and two water tanks altogether.

It was originally a camp fenced in with animals.

The science lab was the pump house.

The long building where I now teach was prayed into existence five years ago – along with all the other buildings now.

The children and Kim would stand on all the corners and sides of the area we needed the building to be and prayed.......

Then the money came in and we progressed with the building. Each Friday Kim would tell the workers that was their last day of work unless more money came in to continue. Each Monday she called workers "Come, we have enough money to continue till Friday." In a month the building was up, and people had contributed enough desks, etc. to furnish with, so children could be taught.

God always provided – always faithful.

About this time, I was courted and married my husband. My husband and I met at a friend's wedding and it was love at first sight.

We married in traditional wedding with only close family members.

He was born in 1958. He was a preacher. His pastorate was at Marikana. I had to continue working. Pastorate was small.

After first baby was born, I still stayed at Dayspring. I slept on Kim's davenport till Kim was going to marry Elijah.

I moved to small room by kitchen. I eventually ended up in small brick house on other side of grassy area, we call our soccer field now.

More children came to Dayspring. A large brick building was constructed. Kim and I talked, and I suggested I be a Hostel Mama. I have 13 children on weekends and 18 during the week.

While I was in small brick house, my husband would come and visit me – he walked and hitchhiked one and a half hours up and back. This was his first pastorate and he wanted me to go with him and support him. It was supported by AFM Church. (Apostles Faith Mission)

This one was three hours away. A rural area. No electricity, no nothing.

He wanted to step out in faith among the underprivileged.

I had to learn to cook using firewood outside. I had to use a wheelbarrow to get water from the nearby river and all that.

Life was so hard and so testing of my faith too.

I got very sick from smoke and strain of work on my body. I was pregnant at this time. Because of hardship I nearly miscarried. So, I had to go back home. He sent me and was so overwhelmed by what he had put me through. He later followed as well. This was not what he had planned, it was not what he expected. He was so disappointed.

He came and took care of our first child, as I had to go to the hospital. That gave me very good bed rest. They constantly were monitoring my baby to see if there would be any complications. I slowly gained strength and was able to leave hospital. After, I had to go for regular checkups though. I eventually gave birth to second daughter.

I had always wanted to obey my husband support him in his vision.

I asked the Lord. "I know I must obey my husband, but I so much miss teaching the little ones. Could you please make a way?"

That's when I became sick. This all happened during winter break – so when school started again, I was able to teach. The Lord was so faithful…….

Through all this Dayspring gave me very good moral support. I was able to teach during this time. It was such a great time for me to be in that association teaching my "little ones". Six of them. I taught them all basic lessons. I was granted a regular maternity leave – three months. I was able to bring my baby to class with me. At that time the rules were more relaxed about that.

My husband would go to his ministry in Wonderkop and would come back two to three times a month.

I was still in small house at this time when I received word that my husband had been attacked!

Three hoodlums had stopped him on his way back from church. He was walking with just his Bible.

They said, "Give me your money!" He had none. "Well, give me your phone then" He had none. "Well then…." Then they stabbed him several times – people saw and heard this and took him to the hospital. They called my phone. Kim and Elijah came with me to main house to phone hospital to see if this was true.

I asked someone to drive me to Rustenburg next day to hospital. I rushed in and doctor told me he had multiple organs seriously injured from stabbing attack.

I went into my husband then and told him not to worry, I would do whatever and take care of him, that I loved him.

He said, "No, don't worry, I am in the hands of the Lord."

I again reassured him I would do whatever I need to do to take care of him, no matter what!

He said, "You don't worry, I am in the Lord's hands".

I said "okay" and we talked a bit more and I told him "goodbye: and I would be back the next day and I left then.

Early the next morning the hospital called. Told me my husband had died.

I didn't want to cry in front of the children (I took care of 16 plus my two) so, I went into the field by my house and cried out to the Lord "Please help me" I lifted my hands and asked "How am I going to take care of my children all alone? Please help me, give me direction, a word!" At that moment, I felt the Lord's hands on my shoulders and reassured me "I will help you, I will always be with you".

Then I was able to go into the house and tell my children.

Then I went to main house, (I didn't go in as I didn't know how a widow should do it, what is appropriate, so I waited outside.)

I called the main house and told Kedi and Esther I had 'news' of my husband. They welcomed me. I told them of my husband's death. We cried and hugged each other.

The next day I went to the hospital and viewed the body and took care of funeral arrangements.

I came back to Dayspring then so I could organize my children, so I could go and bury my husband.

I got volunteer rides the next week so I could go to family grave site. Worship memorial service was held. Ruthie (oldest child) wanted to sing for her Daddy, I asked her, "Do you think you can really do this?" She said yes and she did beautifully. Next day was when we would bury him.

The next day his family release me so I could back to Dayspring and my family. The funeral was done and now back to my daily routine.

My father passed on in April 2013 and my husband passed on in May 2013. After my father died in April of 2013 it was a week later my mother had a stroke and at that time it was decided to put her into a care facility. There she stayed for a while. Later I decided to bring her home with me. I was emotionally strong to do it now. My mom is now 87 years old.

The goodness of the Lord has always been visible and felt. When dealing with my husband's share of the land, He was there.

I rented out the land so it would help with my children's education.

When I became 'house mother' in the hostel, I had 16 children there plus mine. Then my Mama came to live with us – all before my husband died. God's timing is perfect, again.

Then, as now, all children have their own bed and assigned jobs each day.

In the last seven years I have seen the goodness of the Lord, physically and emotionally.

In my low times He always sends someone to come alongside me to lift me up. He has never left me.

I always have the full support of my little family and I do the same for them.

We understand each other and when disputes arrive, we are always able to sit down and work it all out.

So, for me, I feel I am just Blessed!

I forgot to tell you – after my husband died, I took my father's advice and I took driver's training and purchased my own car – a "Tucson".

I praise the Lord!!!!

I know my story isn't done yet, but I continue to praise and trust the Lord in all things – even those I don't understand yet.

Sesi

Photo of long building is the one the children and staff stood around the area they wanted the building to go up in and they prayed it into existence. This is the building that Sesi teaches in. The picture on the right is 'FourSquare'. Bottom left is Sesi's class.

The picture of elephants and zebras are in the nearby animal sanctuary.

One of the pictures is of Sesi and her daughters. (Sesi has a pink dress on)

The long brick building with the three white doors and ventilators on the roof on the right side is where Sesi lives and is house mother to 18 children.

This photo is Sesi in the pink dress with the directors of
the school. The sign above the directors says
"Death could not hold Him down. Jesus is alive."

10-foot-high section of fence around all of Dayspring

Every morning I woke up and praised the Lord for allowing me to see this firsthand

The "Dynamic Duo" Cooks

Principal Uncle Sibanda

Sesi, Author and Sara

Both Dans admiring their handiwork on the new picnic tables.
Notice the artwork on the hostels in the background

Computer room at Dayspring School

Cynthia, a teacher, going over class plans

Mama Mapolo's class

Mercy, head cook, showing one of the bags of food she uses to prepare a meal

School children enjoying their meal to the max

01/27/2020 00:49

School children taking a break in FourSquare. Note in the background the base of the water tank structure where the killer bees have taken up residence

Josie, one of the staff, taking a tea break

Kim, the director, discussing with her husband, Elijah, some management projects

Kim, the director, is labeling and handing out gifts from
Fish Lake Church, Prior Lake, Minnesota

This is Beauty, one of the all-around helpers at the school

Part of Pastor Dan's crew including his twin
granddaughters, much to the children's delight

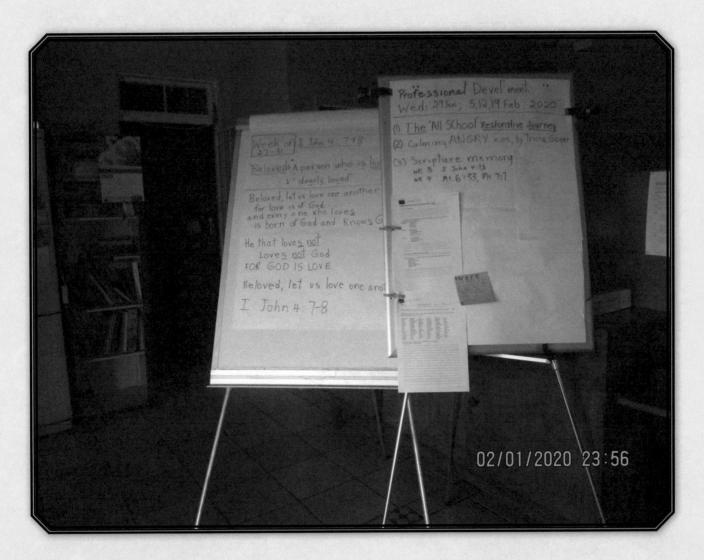

Motto for the class that teacher Barb was teaching. All the classes memorized this

Outdoor study area

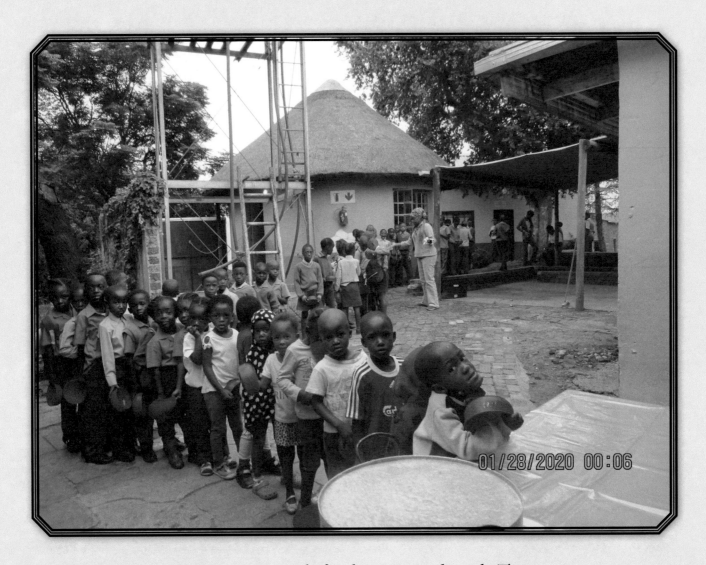

Trying to wait patiently for the next good meal. They are
directed in the background by Beauty in the blue coat,

Uncle Nik, the Africanis Language teacher with a student

Uncle Will (fellow teacher on left) with Pastor Dan from the United States

All the meals were prepared in these kettles by the 'Dynamic Duo'

Awards Day for all the children. Principal Uncle Sibanda is giving instructions

Barb's husband, Dave, standing

01/27/2020 01:06

Sesi and another member of 'the group' discussing plans

Sesi is delighted with the gifts from Fish Lake Church, Prior Lake, Minnesota

Some of Pastor Dan's crew from the United States

Esther, one of the staff, taking a break from computer work to have her tea

02/01/2020 23:05

GoGo in Africanis means Grandma. It's a title of honor there

Growing vegetables for use in feeding the children at the school

Some of the older children waiting for their mealtime

Tammy using her Picasso skills on the picnic tables

Team members making plans to get to the top water tank to dispatch the killer bees

Printed in the United States
By Bookmasters